Weekly Reader Books presents

Heroes of the Revolution

Thomas Jefferson

By Susan & John Lee

Illustrated by Tom Dunnington

 CHILDRENS PRESS, CHICAGO

This book is a presentation of Weekly Reader Books.
Weekly Reader Books offers book clubs for children from
preschool to young adulthood.

For further information write to:
Weekly Reader Books
1250 Fairwood Ave.
Columbus, Ohio 43216

Library of Congress Cataloging in Publication Data

Lee, Susan.
  Thomas Jefferson.

  (Heroes of the Revolution)
  SUMMARY: A biography of the Virginian who was noted
as a statesman, inventor, and author of the Declaration
of Independence.
  1. Jefferson, Thomas, Pres. U.S., 1743-1826—
Juvenile literature. [1. Jefferson, Thomas, Pres.
U.S., 1743-1826. 2. Presidents] I. Lee, John, joint
author. II. Dunnington, Tom, illus. III. Title.
E332.79.L43   973.4′6′0924 [B] [92] 73-17443
ISBN 0-516-04652-7

Birthdays are fun. We like it when other people remember our birthday. Americans take a holiday on the birthdays of two of our greatest Presidents.

This story is about a man who became President. Most Americans don't remember his birthday, but because of him we remember the birthday of our country.

Today Americans live in big cities or in towns near big cities. Very few people live on farms. America has not always been a land of big cities. For a long time, America was a land of farmers.

There was no United States of America two hundred years ago. There were thirteen colonies, each with its own name. These colonies belonged to England, and the King of England ruled over them.

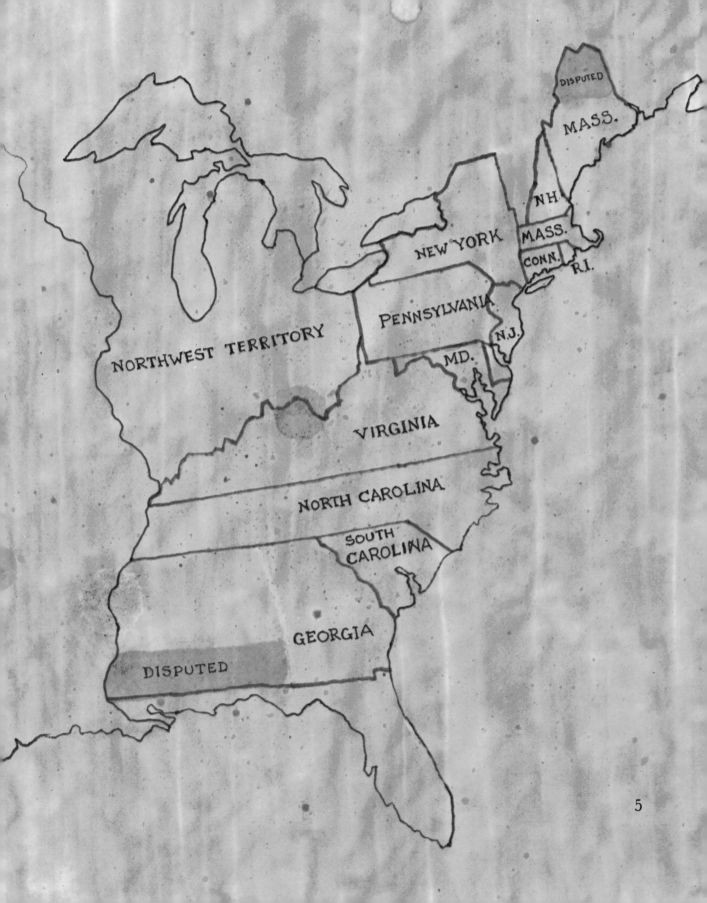

DISPUTED

MASS.

NH

MASS.

CONN.

R.I.

NEW YORK

PENNSYLVANIA

N.J.

MD.

NORTHWEST TERRITORY

VIRGINIA

NORTH CAROLINA

SOUTH CAROLINA

GEORGIA

DISPUTED

5

One of the richest colonies was Virginia. The people of Virginia made money growing tobacco and rice.

The first Virginians farmed the land along the rivers that ran into the Atlantic Ocean. The colonists who came later moved west to find new lands to farm.

If a family had only a little land, their land was called a farm. They were called farmers. Farmers did their own work or had only one or two helpers.

If a family had a lot of land, their land was called a plantation. They were called planters. Planters had slaves and many others who worked for them.

A Virginian by the name of Peter
Jefferson had a plantation far from the
Atlantic Ocean. The woods near the
plantation were full of deer and wolves and
other animals. A tribe of Indians lived near
the plantation.

In April of 1743 the first son of Peter Jefferson and his wife Jane was born. They named him Thomas Jefferson.

The boy began school at the age of five. He, his sisters, and his cousins learned reading, writing, and arithmetic in a one-room schoolhouse on the plantation. Thomas' father owned the school and paid the teacher.

When school was out for the day, Tom
and his friends loved to go hunting in the
mountains. Sometimes they shot a fox or a
wild turkey. Tom learned to ride as a boy.
He liked to ride on the plantation and in
the woods.

When Tom was 14, his father died. Tom had seven brothers and sisters who were still young. Tom stayed in school because he wanted to learn about many different things and ideas.

At 17, Thomas was ready to go to college. He was a tall, thin young man. He had big hands and feet. His hair was red. He had freckles all over his face.

Tom looked like a farmer from the frontier. That is just what he was—a western boy looking for something more than farming or planting.

While Thomas was at the College of
William and Mary, he made up his mind
to study law. When he was 24 years old,
Thomas Jefferson was ready to be a lawyer.

It was not long before the people of
Virginia got to know this tall young lawyer.
In 1769 they elected him to be their
representative to the legislature.

HOUSE OF BURGESSES

Thomas went to the Virginia capital at
Williamsburg to work. The legislature
made the laws for the colony of Virginia.

Jefferson had been elected to the
legislature at an important time. Many
people in the colonies were not happy with
the way England ruled them. They did not
like the taxes that England made them pay.

In Virginia, Patrick Henry was a leader of
people who didn't like English taxes.
Jefferson agreed with Patrick Henry, and
the men soon became friends.

Jefferson also did not like the English idea of keeping the Virginia settlers from moving to the west. The English wanted the Indians to be left alone in the west. Jefferson thought that new colonists should be able to move west and own their farms.

Matters between the colonies and England got worse and worse. In April of 1775, some British soldiers and some Massachusetts colonists got into a fight. Some of the colonies got ready for war.

In Virginia, Jefferson was elected to go
to Philadelphia for a meeting—called a
Congress—with representatives from the
other twelve colonies. At age 32, Thomas
Jefferson was one of the youngest members
of this Congress.

The Congress had many jobs to do. First, it made George Washington head of the army. The Congress also set up a navy. Each of the colonies was told to set up its own government.

The fighting went on between the colonists and the English. More and more people wanted to be free from England.

In June of 1776 a Virginian named Richard Henry Lee stood up in Congress. He asked Congress to say the colonies were united and free of England. The Congress talked about this idea. They thought Lee was right.

Five men were asked to write a
declaration of independence. Among the
men were Thomas Jefferson, John Adams,
and Benjamin Franklin.

Thomas Jefferson wrote this declaration for the Congress. He put many ideas into it. One important idea said that all men are created equal. Jefferson said that all people had the right to life, liberty, and the pursuit of happiness.

He also wrote that people had the right to make their own governments. If a government did not protect the people, then the people had the right to make a new government.

In 1776, these ideas were very new. In most countries in the world, people did not believe all men were equal. They did not think that any one person was just as good as another.

The representatives in the Congress liked the Declaration of Independence. They voted on July 4, 1776 to let everyone know the colonies were united and independent of England.

IN CONGRESS, July 4, 1770

The unanimous Declaration of the thirteen united States of America,

When in the Course of human events, it becomes necessary for one people to dissolve the political bands which have connected them with another, and to assume among the powers of the earth, the separate and equal station to which the Laws of Nature and of Nature's God entitle them, a decent respect to the opinions of mankind requires that they should declare the causes which impel them to the separation. — We hold these truths to be self-evident, that all men are created equal, that they are endowed by their Creator with certain unalienable Rights, that among these are Life, Liberty, and the pursuit of Happiness. — That to secure these rights, Governments are instituted among Men, deriving their just powers from the consent of the governed, — That whenever any Form of Government becomes destructive of these ends, it is the Right of the People to alter or to abolish it, and to institute new Government, laying its foundation on such principles and organizing its powers in such form, as to them shall seem most likely to effect their Safety and Happiness. Prudence, indeed, will dictate that Governments long established should not be changed for light and transient causes; and accordingly all experience hath shewn, that mankind are more disposed to suffer, while evils are sufferable, than to right themselves by abolishing the forms to which they are accustomed. But when a long train of abuses and usurpations, pursuing invariably the same Object evinces a design to reduce them under absolute Despotism, it is their right, it is their duty, to throw off such Government, and to provide new Guards for their future security. — Such has been the patient sufferance of these Colonies; and such is now the necessity which constrains them to alter their former Systems of Government. The history of the present King of Great Britain is a history of repeated injuries and usurpations, all having in direct object the establishment of an absolute Tyranny over these States. To prove this, let Facts be submitted to a candid world. — He has refused his Assent to Laws, the most wholesome and necessary for the public good. — He has forbidden his Governors to pass Laws of immediate and pressing importance, unless suspended in their operation till his Assent should be obtained; and when so suspended, he has utterly neglected to attend to them. — He has refused to pass other Laws for the accommodation of large districts of people, unless those people would relinquish the right of Representation in the Legislature, a right inestimable to them and formidable to tyrants only. — He has called together legislative bodies at places unusual, uncomfortable, and distant from the depository of their public Records, for the sole purpose of fatiguing them into compliance with his measures. — He has dissolved Representative Houses repeatedly, for opposing with manly firmness his invasions on the rights of the people. — He has refused for a long time, after such dissolutions, to cause others to be elected; whereby the Legislative powers, incapable of Annihilation, have returned to the People at large for their exercise; the State remaining in the mean time exposed to all the dangers of invasion from without, and convulsions within. — He has endeavoured to prevent the population of these States; for that purpose obstructing the Laws for Naturalization of Foreigners; refusing to pass others to encourage their migrations hither, and raising the conditions of new Appropriations of Lands. — He has obstructed the Administration of Justice, by refusing his Assent to Laws for establishing judiciary powers. — He has made Judges dependent on his Will alone, for the tenure of their offices, and the amount and payment of their salaries. — He has erected a multitude of New Offices, and sent hither swarms of Officers to harrass our people, and eat out their substance. — He has kept among us, in times of peace, Standing Armies without the Consent of our legislatures. — He has affected to render the Military independent of and superior to the Civil power. — He has combined with others to subject us to a jurisdiction foreign to our constitution, and unacknowledged by our laws; giving his Assent to their Acts of pretended Legislation: — For Quartering large bodies of armed troops among us: — For protecting them, by a mock Trial, from punishment for any Murders which they should commit on the Inhabitants of these States: — For cutting off our Trade with all parts of the world: — For imposing Taxes on us without our Consent: — For depriving us in many cases, of the benefits of Trial by jury: — For transporting us beyond Seas to be tried for pretended offences: — For abolishing the free System of English Laws in a neighbouring Province, establishing therein an Arbitrary government, and enlarging its Boundaries so as to render it at once an example and fit instrument for introducing the same absolute rule into these Colonies: — For taking away our Charters, abolishing our most valuable Laws, and altering fundamentally the Forms of our Governments: — For suspending our own Legislatures, and declaring themselves invested with Power to legislate for us in all cases whatsoever. — He has abdicated Government here, by declaring us out of his Protection and waging War against us. — He has plundered our seas, ravaged our Coasts, burnt our towns, and destroyed the Lives of our people. — He is at this time transporting large Armies of foreign Mercenaries to compleat the works of death, desolation and tyranny, already begun with circumstances of Cruelty & perfidy scarcely paralleled in the most barbarous ages, and totally unworthy the Head of a civilized nation. — He has constrained our fellow Citizens taken Captive on the high Seas to bear Arms against their Country, to become the executioners of their friends and Brethren, or to fall themselves by their Hands. — He has excited domestic insurrections amongst us, and has endeavoured to bring on the inhabitants of our frontiers, the merciless Indian Savages, whose known rule of warfare, is an undistinguished destruction of all ages, sexes and conditions. In every stage of these Oppressions We have Petitioned for Redress in the most humble terms: Our repeated Petitions have been answered only by repeated injury. A Prince whose character is thus marked by every act which may define a Tyrant, is unfit to be the ruler of a free people. Nor have We been wanting in attentions to our British brethren. We have warned them from time to time of attempts by their legislature to extend an unwarrantable jurisdiction over us. We have reminded them of the circumstances of our emigration and settlement here. We have appealed to their native justice and magnanimity, and we have conjured them by the ties of our common kindred to disavow these usurpations, which would inevitably interrupt our connections and correspondence. They too have been deaf to the voice of justice and of consanguinity. We must, therefore, acquiesce in the necessity, which denounces our Separation, and hold them, as we hold the rest of mankind, Enemies in War, in Peace Friends. —

We, therefore, the Representatives of the united States of America, in General Congress, Assembled, appealing to the Supreme Judge of the world for the rectitude of our intentions, do, in the Name, and by Authority of the good People of these Colonies, solemnly publish and declare, That these United Colonies are, and of Right ought to be Free and Independent States; that they are Absolved from all Allegiance to the British Crown, and that all political connection between them and the State of Great Britain, is and ought to be totally dissolved; and that as Free and Independent States, they have full Power to levy War, conclude Peace, contract Alliances, establish Commerce, and to do all other Acts and Things which Independent States may of right do. — And for the support of this Declaration, with a firm reliance on the protection of divine Providence, we mutually pledge to each other our Lives, our Fortunes and our sacred Honor.

Button Gwinnett
Lyman Hall
Geo Walton.

Wm Hooper
Joseph Hewes,
John Penn

Edward Rutledge.

Thos. Heyward Junr.
Thomas Lynch Junr.
Arthur Middleton

John Hancock

Robt Morris
Benjamin Rush
Benj. Franklin
John Morton
Geo Clymer
Jas. Smith.
Geo. Taylor
James Wilson
Geo. Ross

Samuel Chase
Wm. Paca
Thos. Stone
Charles Carroll of Carrollton

George Wythe
Richard Henry Lee
Th Jefferson
Benj. Harrison
Thos. Nelson jr.
Francis Lightfoot Lee
Carter Braxton

Caesar Rodney
Geo Read
Tho M:Kean

Wm Floyd
Phil. Livingston
Frans. Lewis
Lewis Morris

Rich. Stockton
Jno Witherspoon
Fras. Hopkinson
John Hart
Abra Clark

Josiah Bartlett
Wm Whipple
Saml Adams
John Adams
Robt Treat Paine
Elbridge Gerry
Step Hopkins
William Ellery
Roger Sherman
Saml Huntington
Wm Williams
Oliver Wolcott
Matthew Thornton

When the Declaration of Independence
was read to the colonists, they cheered.
Bells rang all over the city of Philadelphia.

Many colonists liked the idea of equality. They did not want to be ruled by England. They wanted to rule themselves. They wanted to be independent of England.

After writing the Declaration of Independence, Thomas Jefferson went back to Virginia. He wanted to help Virginia become a new state. He helped to bring about many changes.

He helped write laws letting each person decide what religion he wanted to be. No one else could tell a person what religion to believe in. He helped start free schools for all children.

One idea of Jefferson's did not work. He wanted to end slavery. He owned slaves who worked on his plantation, but he did not like the idea of slavery. He wanted all Virginians to give up owning slaves.

Many people, however, did not want to go along with Jefferson's plan. In the end, Jefferson kept most of his slaves and only freed a few.

By now, Jefferson was known to most Virginians. He had good ideas, and the Virginians liked most of them. In 1779, Jefferson was elected governor of Virginia.

It was a bad time to be leader of a state. The war with England went on and on. General Washington did not have all the soldiers he needed. The navy was not as strong as the English navy. The Virginians were afraid because their state did not have a strong army. Most of their soldiers were with George Washington.

In 1781, the new year began with the English landing an army in Virginia. The English army was led by Benedict Arnold. The English navy sailed up the James River and burned the new capital of Richmond. Governor Jefferson had to run for his life.

Then General Cornwallis came up from North Carolina. His 1,500 English soldiers joined the 4,000 men from Arnold's army. The Americans and English fought hard; but neither side could win a big battle.

The English almost caught Governor Jefferson again, but he got away. Then the English fought their way to Yorktown. This place was on the York River near the Atlantic Ocean.

At Yorktown the English were trapped. They fought a good battle but lost. General Cornwallis and his troops gave up to the American Army. This was the last big

battle of the Revolutionary War. There
were more fights in the south and west, but
the war was won at Yorktown.

Eight years after the war began, the
English and Americans signed a treaty.
The English said they would send their
army and navy back to England. They said
the colonies were now states and that the
United States were free and independent of
England.

Jefferson was pleased. Now that the war
was over, he planned to spend more time
on his plantation. Since the death of his
wife, his two little girls needed him.

But the new United States also needed a man like Thomas Jefferson. For five years, Jefferson represented the United States in France. Then, in 1789, he agreed to help the first President of the United States, George Washington, with the new government.

Jefferson was elected Vice President in 1796 when John Adams was President. No matter how much he wanted to go back to his home in Virginia, he could never say no to his country.

In 1801, Jefferson was elected the third President of the United States. The nation's capital, Washington, D.C., was so new that many of its roads were muddy and full of holes. The unfinished President's House was covered with a coat of whitewash.

Some people did not like the new President's ways. On the day he became President, Jefferson was living in a simple rooming house. He got up, dressed in a plain suit, and walked to the ceremony. After it, the new President of the United States walked back to his rooming house. All the seats at the table were full when he got there. The President waited until someone was done and then sat down to eat.

Jefferson wanted to act like most other Americans. He did not want to act as if he were better than other people. One visitor to the White House was upset because the President wore old clothes and slippers.

President Jefferson did not want a big
fuss made on his birthday. Two times a
year, on New Year's Day and on the Fourth
of July, he did something special. He
opened the White House to anyone who
wanted to see him or the White House.

When important people came to the
White House for dinner, they ate at a big,
round table. The President said a round
table was a democratic table. It didn't have
a head or a foot for the two most important
people. Everyone was equal at a round
table. He liked to keep things simple.

One of the most important things Jefferson did as President was to buy more land to add to the new nation. For fifteen million dollars, he bought a huge chunk of land between the Mississippi River and the Rocky Mountains. The land he bought from France was called Louisiana.

After America bought Louisiana from France, it had twice as much land as it had before. Many Americans were happy. Now they could move west of the Mississippi River. More Americans could own their own land.

Jefferson had always been interested in western lands. He was born in the west, but now there would be a new west in the United States. He wanted to know about the new lands and find out about the people who lived in them.

He picked two men, William Clark and Meriwether Lewis, to explore the new west. These men led others in exploring this wild, new part of the United States.

Lewis and Clark were gone for almost three years. They went up the Missouri River to its beginnings. Next they crossed the Rocky Mountains. Then they went down the Columbia River to the Pacific Ocean.

LOUISIANA
PURCHASE

Along the way they made many useful maps. They met all kinds of Indians. The men also brought back different types of soil, plants, and Indian tools. They even brought back two bear cubs which Jefferson kept on the White House lawn. Lewis and Clark were good explorers and scientists.

President Jefferson had no trouble getting elected again in 1805. He had more problems than he had before. France and England were at war with each other.

The United States wanted to stay out of the fight. But the English stopped

American ships. They took American sailors off these ships and made them work on English ships. In June of 1807, the English even fired on an American warship, the *Chesapeake*.

President Jefferson stopped American ships from sailing to other nations. Many sailors lost their jobs because there was no work for them. Merchants went out of business because they could not sell their goods in Europe. Many people did not like Jefferson for this, but America did not get into the war while he was President.

MONTICELLO

In 1809, Jefferson returned to his Virginia home, which he called Monticello. He was a planter again. He worked in his gardens and fields. He ordered many different kinds of seeds from Europe. He wanted to see if they would grow in Virginia soil.

CANNON BALL CLOCK

Jefferson also fixed up his home. Visitors went away talking about the things Jefferson had invented. He made a seven-day calendar clock run by cannon balls. In his house were many things he made, a revolving chair and desk, a revolving buffet, and a four-sided music stand. He liked showing his house and plantation to the many people who came to see him.

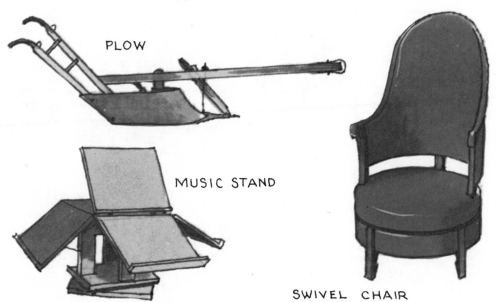

PLOW

MUSIC STAND

SWIVEL CHAIR

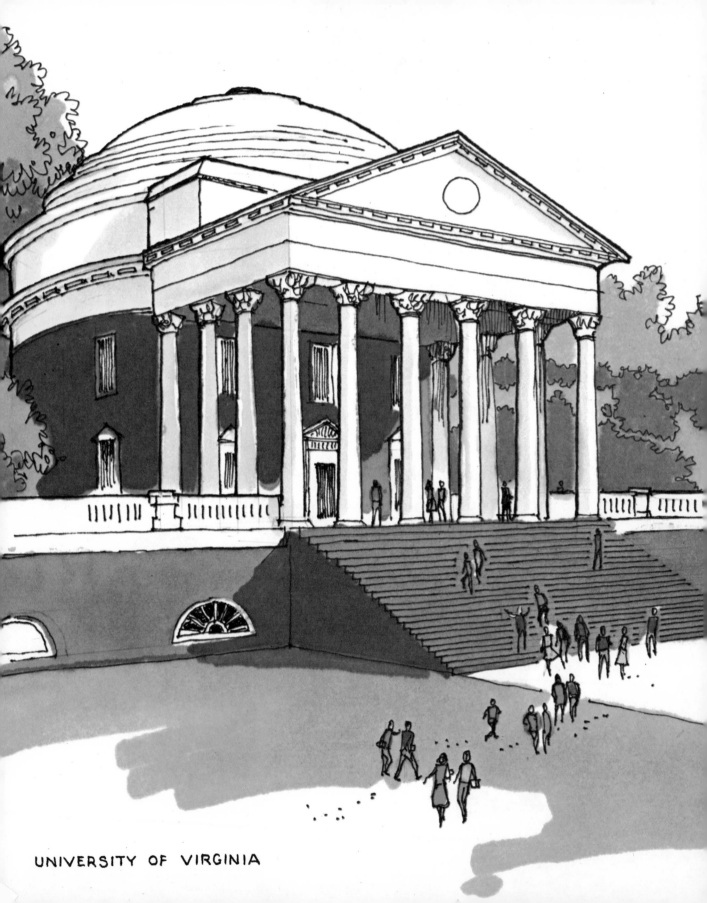

UNIVERSITY OF VIRGINIA

Near the end of his life, Jefferson helped start the University of Virginia. He helped draw the plans for the buildings. He helped plan what people could study there. He helped pick books to go in the new library.

Jefferson thought an education was important for staying free. He thought every citizen should have a good education. He worked on plans for the University of Virginia almost until the time he died.

Thomas Jefferson died on July 4, 1826. He was 83 years old. The man who wrote the Declaration of Independence died on its 50th birthday. We do not have a holiday for Jefferson's birthday. But every Fourth of July we have a holiday to remember the declaration he wrote.

About the Authors:

Susan Dye Lee has been writing professionally since she graduated from college in 1961. Working with the Social Studies Curriculum Center at Northwestern University, she has created course materials in American studies. Ms. Lee has also co-authored a text on Latin America and Canada, written case studies in legal history for the Law in American Society Project, and developed a teacher's guide for tapes that explore woman's role in America's past. The writer credits her students for many of her ideas. Currently, she is doing research for her history dissertation on the Women's Christian Temperance Union for Northwestern University. In her free moments, Susan Lee enjoys traveling, playing the piano, and welcoming friends to "Highland Cove," the summer cottage she and her husband, John, share.

John R. Lee enjoys a prolific career as a writer, teacher, and outdoorsman. After receiving his doctorate in social studies at Stanford, Dr. Lee came to Northwestern University's School of Education, where he advises student teachers and directs graduates in training. A versatile writer, Dr. Lee has co-authored the Scott-Foresman social studies textbooks for primary-age children. In addition, he has worked on the production of 50 films and over 100 filmstrips. His biographical film on Helen Keller received a 1970 Venice Film Festival award. His college text, *Teaching Social Studies in the Elementary School*, has recently been published. Besides pro-football, John Lee's passion is his Wisconsin cottage, where he likes to shingle leaky roofs, split wood, and go sailing.

About the Artist:

Tom Dunnington divides his time between book illustration and wildlife painting. He has done many books for Childrens Press, as well as working on textbooks, and is a regular contributor to "Highlights for Children." He is at present working on his "Endangered Wildlife" series, which is being reproduced as limited edition prints. Tom lives in Elmhurst, Illinois.